Hermane Chagas
Adriano Barros
Vorster Alves

People Management Models

Hermane Chagas
Adriano Barros
Vorster Alves

People Management Models

Systematic literature review of the main models

ScienciaScripts

Imprint

Cover image: www.ingimage.com

This book is a translation from the original published under ISBN 978-613-9-61584-1.

Publisher:
Sciencia Scripts
is a trademark of
Dodo Books Indian Ocean Ltd. and OmniScriptum S.R.L publishing group

120 High Road, East Finchley, London, N2 9ED, United Kingdom
Str. Armeneasca 28/1, office 1, Chisinau MD-2012, Republic of Moldova, Europe
Printed at: see last page
ISBN: 978-620-7-87053-0

Table of contents:

CENTER FOR HIGHER EDUCATION AND DEVELOPMENT
FACULTY OF APPLIED SOCIAL SCIENCES
SPECIALIZED COURSE IN STRATEGIC PEOPLE MANAGEMENT
HÉRMANE JASHER CABRAL DAS CHAGAS
PEOPLE MANAGEMENT MODELS: A SYSTEMATIC REVIEW OF LITERATURE ON THE MAIN MODELS
CAMPINA GRANDE-PB 2016

HÉRMANE JASHER CABRAL DAS CHAGAS

PEOPLE MANAGEMENT MODELS: A SYSTEMATIC LITERATURE REVIEW OF THE MAIN MODELS

Course Conclusion Paper (Monograph) presented as a pre-requisite for obtaining the title of Specialist in Strategic People Management by the Faculty of Applied Social Sciences of Campina Grande- PB.
Area of Concentration: People Management.
Supervisor: Vorster Queiroga Alves

International Cataloging in Publication Data
(Facisa Library)
XXXX

Chagas, Hérmane Jasher Cabral das.

People Management Models: Systematic Literature Review on the main models / Hérmane Jasher Cabral das Chagas. -- Campina Grande, 2016.

Originally presented as a Course Conclusion Paper for the Specialization in Strategic People Management - Qualified in Research by the author (specialist - Faculty of Applied Social Sciences, 2016).
References.
1. monograph. 2. standardization. I. People Management Models: Systematic Literature Review on the main models.

CDU-XXXX

Course Conclusion Paper (Monograph), People Management Models: Systematic Literature Review on the main models, presented by Hérmane Jasher Cabral das Chagas as part of the requirements for obtaining the title of Specialist in Strategic People Management awarded by FACISA - Faculty of Applied Social Sciences of Campina Grande-PB.

APPROVED IN ______/ ____ / ____

EXAMINING BOARD:

ADVISOR'S NOTE: ______

Prof. Vorster Queiroga Alves, Msc.

NOTE FROM THE CO-SUPERVISOR: ______

Prof.ª Elenilze Josefa Diniz, Dr.ª

FINAL NOTE: __________

I dedicate it to my parents, José Francisco das Chagas and Genidalva Cabral das Chagas, for their teachings, and to my wife, Renata Macedo Furtado.

Now give me wisdom and knowledge, that I may go out and come in before this people; for who can judge this great people?" (II Chronicles 1:10).

SUMMARY

With the evolution implied by globalization, through techniques and methods of business management, the task of managing companies has become increasingly complex due to the growth in the range of aspects inherent in the process of managing, especially the people aspect, which becomes from simple operators of standardized procedures to collaborators of knowledge and aggregators of value through continuous improvements, which is why the challenge of managing in a scenario of rapid change is that it is perceived that the answer lies in people and in the application of a model that is efficient and strategic for companies. The general aim of this study is to analyze the People Management models described in the literature, from the publications in the annals of the Revista de Administraçao Contemporánea - RAC over the last five (5) years, from 2010 to 2015, with the aim of showing which models are practiced in Brazilian companies, observing characteristics and forms of application, so that through the definitions studied it is possible to understand the need to apply one or other of these management models in order to make better use of human capital and its potential. The research carried out was a systematic review of the literature, of an exploratory theoretical nature, which made it possible to find the contribution of various authors in the area. It can also be characterized as inductive and explanatory, with qualitative and quantitative approaches, so that it was possible to extract characteristics of these models that would make it possible to categorize the articles collected and classified among the models existing in the theories. The analysis and discussion made it possible to see that there is a concern to practice techniques associated with modern People Management models, which are necessary to meet market demands, but it was also noticed that management methods still need to be consolidated and applied over the long term, through a sustainable vision and linked to strategic planning as one of the main premises for companies to survive.

Keywords: People Management. People Management Models. Competitive Management.

Chapter 1

1 INTRODUCTION

Business competitiveness has led companies to invest more and more in the processes inherent in the production of goods and services, as well as in human capital, which is a fundamental element in the organization's development process. This makes it necessary for companies to invest in management tools, with regard to Human Resources Management, which, according to Xavier (2006), the constant changes are the major barriers to be overcome, changes which are exhaustively faced, but which are always occurring, in one way or another, highlighting the permanent challenge to be overcome day after day by companies.

The changes that have taken place in the administrative management of companies as a result of globalization, especially in the economic, technological and information fields, have influenced managers to adopt and formulate ideas for managing human capital. According to Fischer (2002), in the course of change, the organization must be aware of its actions, as they need to be objective, clear and supported by participatory management and a high level of interaction between members.

In this sense, managers must understand that business changes and strategies must involve people, because according to Barbosa and Estender (2014, p.1) "People management focuses on the coexistence of human beings, because it is there that employees spend most of their lives, providing their services". It is necessary to understand that organizations are characterized by the existence of people, with common objectives, even with their particularities. It is therefore important for managers to work concisely with the main element that drives an institution, which is people.

In this respect, Ribeiro (2005) argues that information, due to its flow and use, makes people within the organization increasingly important, as they are the ones who handle and make strategic use of knowledge. Organizations are increasingly realizing that people, as strategic partners, are fundamental resources for achieving the company's objectives. Faria (2006, p. 11) states that "man must be considered, in all his complexity, as someone who thinks, reflects, produces new ideas and is capable of bringing about change". In other words, the presence and participation of people in companies needs to be managed, guided and satisfied, as they are the most expensive and difficult resources to manage.

In this way, considering that it is a topic explored by scholars on the subject, but also realizing the evolution of complexity in people management today, we seek to collaborate, through a study of existing people and organizational management models, to observe the appropriate types that can be effectively applied or adjusted to reality.

Complementing the importance of people management, Sinek (2012) was very assertive when he once said that it is not possible for the customers of a particular company to like it if, first of all, the employees do not understand it.

Therefore, it can be seen that people make all the difference within organizations and that the management of internal factors so that this resource contributes positively, influencing changes and improvements, must take place in a very well aligned manner, but only when the scenario is conducive to this, which according to Ulrich (2012), there is a possibility that people will present certain unfeasible postures for improvements in companies, but that this is also part of this work of managing people in organizations.

Considering the points made above and understanding that it is essential for people to be allocated and directed in the most appropriate way, through efficient management (People Management), we realize that it is critical to study and clarify the existing people management models, in order to understand their relevance to the present day.

Therefore, the challenge of understanding and explaining how to manage an organization in a context full of adversities is that we realize that the answer lies in people and in the application of a model that is efficient and strategic for companies. With this in mind, the following question was asked: **What are the main People Management models found in scientific publications over the last five years?**

The aim of this paper is to analyze the People Management models described in the scientific literature, from the publications in the annals of the Revista de Administragao Contemporánea - RAC over the last five (5) years, from 2010 to 2015. To this end, this material, based on a systematic literature review, aimed to systematize theories on people and organization management; identify existing people management models and report on the main characteristics of the management models found.

Chapter 2

2 THEORETICAL FRAMEWORK

2.1 PEOPLE MANAGEMENT

In the world of organizations, there has always been a dependence on people acting within and/or for them, a situation that has always been circumvented with operational and even managerial practices. The passage of time has meant that this relationship, as well as the internal relationships within the company, have become something to be controlled more efficiently, not only through the necessary labour practices, but also through action concerned with the management of factors, understanding that people are one of the organization's resources (FARIA, 2006). Nowadays, the understanding is that companies and their managers no longer see people as resources, but rather as partners, who can contribute and are essentially strategic in achieving organizational goals.

Ribeiro (2005) shared that studies show that a reality generally seen in Brazilian companies is that the human resources sector, which is responsible for managing people in organizations, is not properly exploited, and its potential remains untapped due to the lack of understanding that this management can provide for the achievement of goals if it is well aligned with the strategic planning outlined by the company.

However, according to the same author's contribution, it is important to stress that the "Human Resources" function is no longer simply involved in bureaucratic and formal processes, such as recruitment, selection and personnel department processes, but has a strategic role, which can take place as long as people management truly takes place within organizations, making it possible to develop measures to develop people's individual talents and help create a corporate environment in which everyone participates and contributes (RIBEIRO, 2005).

Considering these lines of thought and critical analyses of the potential of the "Human Resources" sector, according to Faria's (2006) contribution, People Management can be understood as a set of methods that aim to help managers carry out their activities through the people who make up their team, executing tasks in order to achieve individual and organizational goals.

As a complementary form of definition, Teiga (2012) defines people management as the aggregation of administrative methods, policies, techniques and even practices, with the aim of managing conduct, performance and inherent aspects to optimize the performance of people in the organization.

Finally, according to Ribeiro (2005), it is important to know that for people management to be properly implemented, it must operate according to certain internal processes that are necessary for its function to be active and effective in the organization. These processes will be described in the following topics.

2.2 PEOPLE MANAGEMENT OBJECTIVES

Every organization has a purpose, a mission, a vision, which will define the purpose of its existence and this makes it possible to clarify and set organizational goals, year after year, through strategic planning work that must be carried out, monitored and reviewed, in other words, the company's objective must be challenging and clear. However, for people management, the objectives must be aligned and delimited in accordance with the goals strategically set by the organization, which is why Ulrich (2003) contributes by saying in general terms that the objectives of people management must always be:

a) Helping the company achieve its goals and objectives;
b) Boost the company's competitiveness;
c) Providing well-trained and motivated employees for the company;
d) Developing the achievement of employees' personal expectations in the workplace;
e) Creating and improving the quality of life in the organization's environment;
f) To administer ethical policies and practices that promote a social profile focused on honesty and professional integrity.

But, according to the same author, People Management has both operational and strategic roles, considering the context of action on two fronts, processes and people, as shown in figure 1 below.

Figure 1 - Responsibilities of People Management

Source: ÁVILA and STECCA (2015)

Ulrich (2003) puts it somewhat paradoxically, but in practice it makes perfect sense, because of the perception that on the vertical axis, people management can be strategic when it is well defined with goals to be achieved and with activities aimed at the long term, while its participation in the operational focus is due to the routines of human resources activities themselves, with daily participation. As for the horizontal axis, people management will have to contribute from the operation itself, through administrative routines and the use of bureaucratic tools and practices, to the involvement and influence on people's behavior, acting cooperatively with employees to create a suitable, productive and motivating environment.

2.3 PEOPLE MANAGEMENT PROCESSES

In these definitions it is understood that in People Management there are some necessary and standardized processes in organizations with a serious management, and these processes are defined in (XAVIER, 2006):

a) Adding People: this is defined simply by the activities of recruiting and selecting staff, and is responsible for bringing in new employees who have a very assertive alignment with the "competencies" required by the company;
b) Applying People: is linked to the definition of people's delegations within the organization and is defined by the activities of work modeling and performance evaluation, which are respectively associated with the responsibilities of formally and informally defining the activities to be performed in that function and position, finally performance evaluation is a method, which uses one or more tools to evaluate the level of operational and even behavioral performance achieved by the employee;
c) Rewarding People: is linked to the aspect of remuneration, generally direct and indirect, as it is divided into two activities as well, which are rewards/remuneration and benefits/services;
d) Developing People: this is a relatively new process that is constantly being improved in organizations. It is divided into three activities such as training and development, change programs and communication programs. The practice of developing people is a process that, used strategically, can leverage great results from the people who make up the organization, as it allows for the technical as well as the behavioral development of employees;
e) Keeping People: this process is not of interest to all organizations, since some simply accept the "turnover" of the market or of their own public of employees, defined by the nature of the business in which the company is inserted or even by the fact of the new "trends" of the new generations, but this process when implemented it follows the activities of benefits and job description and analysis, it also becomes strategic when associated with a practice that can arise from the strategic planning of the organization which is the strategic planning of people, observing the critical functions and positions of the organization;
f) Monitoring People: this last process is generally used with administrative and/or senior management teams, with the aim of monitoring the various aspects that link people to organizations, which occurs through management information system and database activities.

People Management processes emerged with the need for a Human Resources sector in organizations, with the basic objective of meeting labor, departmental and purely operational demands, and from their inception to the present day these processes have not undergone major adjustments, But what has happened is that these processes have become associated with new practices in the HR sector, going beyond simply fulfilling routine tasks, which only met the basic demands of the sector, and then taking on increasingly strategic roles within organizations, acting as an extremely important helper and agent for true People Management.

2.4 NEW CONCERNS IN PEOPLE MANAGEMENT

These would be new processes or activities that are necessary and demanded by the growing challenges of the new context experienced by people management, which Faria (2006), also concerned about this scenario of change, said that organizations do not understand that they have the necessary resources to overcome any challenge determined by the changes in the market, it is enough to develop innovative management techniques, but there is no talk of directly managing financial, material and other resources, but of giving priority to employees who play an important role in helping companies to overcome market adversities.

Equally concerned about this issue, Xavier (2006) also states that businesspeople need to understand that it is increasingly necessary to place the "Human Resources" functions, with the strategic contribution of People Management, as closely linked as possible to strategic planning and objectives, otherwise there is no point, for example, in developing functional systems, systems without involving the people of the organization, because if this integration is done well and the inclusion is effective, any and all gaps that occur or arise will have the contribution of people to the improvement in order to make any development sustainable within the organization.

According to Xavier (2006), in the modern world, which is increasingly complex due to its diversity, there are some aspects that should be worked on as soon as possible:

a) Social composition of teams: experiences, ages, genders, education levels, create a very diverse environment that can make management complicated, but at the same time creates opportunities to use diverse talents;
b) Individual values: opinions, beliefs, political positions, social ideologies have never been more exposed than today, which also allows the opportunity to use the various positions put forward to encompass ever more innovative ideas for solving problems;
c) Lifestyles: the exposure and existence, to a greater extent than before, of new preferences allows cooperative participation with more visions for exploring the world;
d) People's professional training and orientation: the widespread dissemination of information and knowledge that occurs today has created a society with increasingly specialized and in-depth training, which makes it possible to form teams with diverse individual knowledge, but which together allow for greater exploration of detail in solving problems in various spheres

of knowledge.

Therefore, it is clear that the solution to any innovative challenge, internal or external problem, random market adversity, lies in the people who make up the company. They can generate problems because of their intrinsic particularities, but they are also the factors that will enable the solution to each problem. It will be even more assertive if People Management tries to get to know and understand its employees and practices the best way to involve them in the organization's interests, because the ultimate goal is to apply them in an optimized way with the organization's strategic goals.

2.5 STRATEGIC PEOPLE MANAGEMENT

According to Tachizawa, Ferreira and Fortuna (2001), strategic management is a process of realizing and ensuring, through administrative measures, that previously decided premises are met in order to achieve a long-term competitive stance.

Strategic People Management, according to Fleury and Fleury (2000), is the linking of people management practices and measures to contribute to business strategy. In other words, it is the use of all the potential that efficient people management can bring to bear on the strategic decisions to be made.

An important contribution that Ulrich (2003) made on this subject was when he stated that in many businesses managers have a positive attitude towards the importance and relevance that employees have, but it is perceived in the way these companies are managed that it is not understood how People Management can make their visions of the future a reality.

Therefore, a process of managing people strategically can be a way of operating human resources and even a set of operational practices combined with management methods that go beyond guaranteeing the bureaucratic routines of HR, but add value strategically, making the organization more competitive (ALHO; CARVALHO, 2007).

As will be seen later in this study, among the new practices of managing people there is a model that establishes how to apply methods that make this management strategic for the organization, but there are even more modern proposals these days to create flexibility even for a method like this, making what was thought strategically into flexible means for the changes dictated by the market.

According to Faria (2006), aspects that were previously important separately become fundamental when worked on simultaneously within a strategic approach to people, such as managing the organizational culture as fundamental to the success of the business, technical and behavioural training and development as essential to achieving organizational goals, and managing the organizational climate to keep the team working together, involved and concerned about results.

2.6 PEOPLE MANAGEMENT MODELS

As with any model, People Management models are made up of predefined ways of carrying out the activities required to manage people, but they differ in their particularities and some fundamental aspects (CHIAVENATO, 1999).

These standards, which have been studied and established over time, are now widely used due to the need to apply people management practices that are increasingly based on standardized routines, but in accordance with the needs that people impose on their day-to-day lives within the business environment. Therefore, based on the premise that initial and appropriate models for managing human resources are essential, according to Fischer (2002), it can be reported that for People Management models, as worked on by scholars and proposed over time, they can be divided into two large blocks, which are the Classic or Traditional Models and the New Models or Innovative Models.

These two blocks are mainly differentiated by the period in which they were developed, since the first block of traditional models has been a major milestone in existing management models, where they can be cited as: the classic model, the motivational model, the strategic model and the competitive model (ALHO; CARVALHO, 2007). The second block, characterized by the adaptation to the evolution of organizations and also to the new challenges of the current modernity experienced by the globalized market, is more understood as dimensions that make People Management models flexible, allowing modern organizations to alternate how to apply Human Resources practices and policies in an operational, strategic and competitive way simultaneously.

2.6.1 Traditional models

The traditional models are considered to be the framework for standards of practice and methods applied in a structured way for the effective performance of activities related to people management, such as the bureaucratic practices that the HR sector carries out, but it is also through these traditional models that a more strategic use of HR begins, based on concern for aspects inherent to people that can affect the organization's performance. These models are divided into the classic people management model, the motivational people management model, the strategic people management model and the competitive people management model (ALHO; CARVALHO, 2007).

2.6.1.1 Classic people management model

According to Fischer (2002), this model, which emerged in 1903, was based on the proposals of studies by Frederick Taylor and Henry Ford, where the production capacity of the time did not keep up with growing demand and a characteristic of the time was that the wishes of customers were almost irrelevant. In this way, the model was proposed simply because it was concerned with ensuring that employees were focused on carrying out tasks according to very strict rules and standards in order to achieve maximum productivity, because everything was essentially operational, without worrying about what the worker thought or thought.

Therefore, the basic function of this classic model is simply to provide support for employees to be recruited, taught to perform tasks with a high level of standardization and low cognitive challenge; without concern for social and motivational aspects.

2.6.1.2 Motivational people management model

It emerged as a criticism of the previous model, since the careful and repetitive execution of tasks created an increase in productivity, but also triggered worker dissatisfaction due to the lack of challenges and the absence of learning (ALHO; CARVALHO, 2007).

So, this model is based on the idea that keeping workers motivated and satisfied is also an important factor in keeping productivity high. Therefore, with human relations studies concerned with keeping employees satisfied, investments began to be made in actions that promoted everyone's well-being, changing processes to broader activities to generate a little more challenge, and the first studies on quality of life at work also emerged. Thus, the provision of benefits was a resource that began to be used, as well as management practices that were "concerned" with the situation of employees, but proposed that everyone should feel part of the team (FISCHER, 2002).

2.6.1.3 Strategic people management model

Around 1970, another approach emerged, which can be considered an evolution of the two previous models, because organizations were already achieving very high productivity and there was concern about employee satisfaction, so internally things were under control, but the evolution started from the perception that an organization functions as a large system, made up of several sub-systems, In a similar way to the human body, a model adapted from biology by Ludwig von Bertalanffy, in which internally there is an interaction between these systems influencing each other to achieve a final result and also in the same way that the human body interacts with the external environment, in this model the organization as a system also acts and suffers action from the environment in which it is inserted (ALHO; CARVALHO, 2007).

This new model has revolutionized the way organizations are managed, because in addition to understanding how to better rationalize the practices of the sectors, knowing that there are internal systems, but also that it is necessary to worry about the external environment and this was a vital point, since worrying about the external environment made it possible to understand the needs and demands of consumers, who now became the focus of the companies' services.

In other words, the strategic role that this model proposes to play is precisely that the focus on the customer becomes the guiding principle for the decisions and measures to be taken, which will influence the way organizations and their internal systems are managed.

This brings us to the issue of People Management, since companies now perceive their employees as collaborators, who need to contribute to and get involved with the organization's intentions. This model therefore proposes to continue working to achieve maximum productivity, but at levels acceptable to the market, with internal satisfaction for its workers, who are now considered collaborators, since the company's interest is that they participate in achieving the goals because they understand that this is important for the company and for them (ALHO; CARVALHO, 2007).

2.6.1.4 Competitive people management model

With the understanding that the market was now the target, that it could not produce in large quantities because the customer might not want to consume the good or service produced, organizations soon focused on the customer and this made the market very aggressive, and around 2000 the competitive model emerged to manage organizations in a highly competitive environment (FISCHER, 2002).

According to the same author, the great thing about this model is that it enables organizations to adapt to the current moment dictated by the market, taking into account the various possibilities that may arise (FISCHER, 2002).

So, what is decisive for this model to work in line with People Management is that the importance now lies not only in the concern about the extremely competitive environment, but also in the consequences this has for people within the organization and how they can be put to better use in the company, since they have the potential to bring about change, but only if they are aligned to do so (ALHO; CARVALHO, 2007).

People management now acts in a more strategic way than before, but focused on making the best use of employees, enabling them to be more engaged, developing the knowledge and skills deficits necessary for human potential, because it was necessary to apply people so that in addition to operational and productive application, it was also critical that improvements and innovations took place to make the organization continuously competitive (ULRICH, 2003).

Awareness of responsibilities, personal development, the perception of collaborative potential for improvements, the need to continually evolve processes, and adding intellectual capital to the company are the main characteristics of this competitive people management model (ALHO; CARVALHO, 2007).

2.6.2 New People Management Models

Since the beginning of this work, we have discussed globalization, modern management practices, the influence of people on the internal processes of organizations and people management models, but nothing has yet dealt with modern management proposals that take into account the already discussed characteristics that are inherent to the new way of managing people in the business environment, such as social values, lifestyles and increasingly diverse opinions.

However, studies in this direction have already been outlined and elucidated in order to define existing and already practiced proposals in organizations, so that current people management models themselves can be adapted to increasingly appropriate and applicable options today.

These models, according to Alho and Carvalho (2007), are based on the assumption that models such as strategic and competitive people management form a flexible basis for action in the human resources sector, making it possible to adjust people management activities according to the organization's current needs by exchanging practices from both models.

To this end, Alho and Carvalho (2007) have identified five dimensions, referred to in this paper as new models, for people management. These dimensions characterized by the author determine new proposals for managing people through means such as: competency-based management, strategic change management, organizational climate management, organizational culture management and knowledge and learning management. However, these dimensions operate simultaneously, with greater or lesser proportions of one or other of these practices, allowing for strategic and competitive gains.

2.6.2.1 Competency-based management

As has been mentioned in this article, the constant changes that the market imposes make it almost impossible to apply models that have already been drawn up and proposed for the structure and working methods of teams, since this constant change that takes place in organizations creates the need for dynamic management in order to make proper use of people, In other words, a constant and adjustable use of different people management practices becomes essential, which is why competency management works, as it is a model that makes the most appropriate use of the internal diversity of people's individual potentials to achieve positive results for the organization (ALHO; CARVALHO, 2007).

Corroborating this line of thought, Faria (2006) points out that the basic model for managing people needs to take an approach based on the concept of the team's internal competencies, based precisely on the aspect of the potential that people possess within the organization today, but made possible by the influence that the people management sector now possesses.

The approach of this management model, as mentioned by Faria (2006), is based on the increasingly strong association between organizational strategy and people management, considering it as the management of the most important and critical resource for companies today. In other words, the application of the issue to the area/function that people management has linked to strategic planning.

However, in practice, this model makes a lot of sense when you consider that today's organizations should be seen as a "portfolio of competencies", since the level of education and technical training is much better and the concern is to make optimum use of these skills and knowledge by managing the various capabilities of their employees, managing motivation and efficiently guiding the addition of people to processes (FARIA, 2006).

In this way, it can be said that people's actions must be directed in accordance with the determinations imposed by the market and aligned with organizational strategies, associating that, according to Fleury (2002), these people's actions must be collaborative and cooperative, in order to integrate and create an environment of synergy through the skills and knowledge they can add, converting these aspects into economic value for the company.

To do this, it is important to describe what competence is, which, according to Brandao and Guimaraes (2001), can be described as attributes that individuals possess and that organizations need in order to achieve a competitive advantage, mainly by being able to find differentiated "competences" that create a distinct process or result and that determine characteristics that are difficult to imitate.

In a more enlightening way, Leme (2005) reports that competence is the set of Knowledge, Skills and Attitudes, which can be described as:

a) Knowledge (C): is related to the knowledge that the individual has from accumulated learning from their training and private studies;
b) Skill (H): this aspect is related to knowing how to do things, i.e. it is basically the practice of knowledge that is transformed into action;
c) Attitude (A): the latter relates to the intention to do, or the will to do, which lies between the practice being carried out and knowledge.

Therefore, it can be described in a more objective way that competency-based management is a model characterized by the identification and association of competencies considered essential for a given moment in a company, with the aim of using these as fundamental resources for achieving strategic goals, through the development and efficient application of competencies (ALHO; CARVALHO, 2007).

2.6.2.2 Knowledge and learning management

In general, this model focuses essentially on the aspect of implicit knowledge that people can acquire and apply in practice, as well as the process of assimilating more knowledge that can be strategic for the organization.

Knowledge Management is a managerial process of using, by identifying, renewing and applying the knowledge that exists in the organization's teams and that is strategic for certain processes (NONAKA; TAKEUCHI, 1997).

According to the same authors, it can also be understood as the management of the knowledge resources that the company holds, enabling it to know what it has and doesn't have in the way of strategic skills that are relevant to the context in which it operates. But it is also possible, through this management model, to quantify and evaluate the possibilities for applying the company's knowledge, allowing the best decisions to be made to be defined, as it is possible through this process to be more assertive about the practices to be carried out at the most appropriate time (NONAKA; TAKEUCHI, 1997).

This model and managerial way of dealing with knowledge is due to the fact that modern organizations consider that financial, natural and material resources are not the only ones that make up their assets, but knowledge itself and the possibilities it can generate are also now considered to be a component of an organization's wealth. In fact, according to Alho and Carvalho (2007), knowledge today can be considered a more valuable resource than tangible assets, measured in accounting terms, for a company.

Therefore, according to Alho and Carvalho (2007), a knowledge management process generally follows a sequence of three steps: knowledge acquisition, development, dissemination and construction. This treatment of the knowledge management process is fundamental for the efficient use of this resource, and this sequence generally does not have a standardized model, but rather techniques and practices particular to each organization, which are dealt with through organizational learning.

Organizational learning, according to Fleury and Oliveira Jr. (2002) is not only a cognitive process that occurs through the phenomenon of acquiring knowledge, which takes place at all times within the three stages mentioned by Alho and Carvalho (2007), but this method can also be at three levels that are easily perceived within the organization as follows:

a) Individual level: when learning takes place individually and particularly by theme for each interest;
b) Group level: occurs when learning takes place at the level of common groups within an organization, with the aim of sharing knowledge;
c) Organizational level: at the last level, knowledge sharing occurs throughout the organization, through managed techniques and means, characterized by the institutionalization of knowledge.

2.6.2.3 Strategic management of mindanga

With all the dynamics of the market and the complexities imposed on organizational structures and patterns, it is clear that change is a natural part of the business world and that organizations need to be able to adapt to ever greater levels of flexibility.

Organizational strategies are developed through a meticulous planning process, which tries to take into account the most diverse internal and external possibilities, in order to previously adapt the possibilities that the company will use (CHIAVENATO, 1999).

However, even the changes and strategies that exist to deal with the impositions demanded by the market need to be managed, using techniques or even methods that help to change the company's attitude and internal attitudes. This is why there is Strategic Change Management, which, according to Alho and Carvalho (2007), is a model that offers great competitive potential due to the ability to innovate and adapt to the rapid and constant evolution of society's demands.

In this model, it is important to realize that it is not a simple process, since it involves not only adjustments to internal policies, processes, structures and procedures, but also and especially the behavioral profile of employees and their groups, reaching the level of influencing and being influenced by the organizational culture (ALHO; CARVALHO, 2007).

Strategic management for change occurs efficiently when the organization manages to change its strategic posture in the face of market behavior, moving from a structured initial state to another intended and previously planned state, meeting the performance and cost expectations that are necessary to achieve the expected results (NADLER, 1898 apud Silva and Vergara, 1999).

Therefore, People Management acts concomitantly and essentially throughout the process necessary for the company's adaptation, while strategic management for change is being applied, because critical steps for the successful application of business transformation occur through aspects of human adaptation within the company, which are strategically involved in the entire process of developing the organization's planning.

2.6.2.4 Organizational Culture Management

Initially, we can use the definition of culture, in the broadest sense in the context of organizations, as a set of habits, norms and values established through attitudes and expectations shared, if not by all, but by the majority of the members of an organization.

Thus, according to Chiavenato (2000), "organizational culture is the set of habits, beliefs, values and traditions, interactions and social relationships typical of each organization". The same author tells us that the organization is "a human and complex system, with its own characteristics typical of its culture and organizational climate" (CHIAVENATO, 2000).

With the contribution made by the author and for a better clarification, Alho and Carvalho (2007) also contribute by saying that organizational culture has one main function, which is to disseminate to all employees, customers and suppliers the ethical and professional attitude that the company proposes to work with and conduct its business.

The important fact that links organizational culture with people management is that, according to Alho and Carvalho (2007), cultural aspects of the organization, which guide the various behaviors, are critical and intrinsically linked to the processes of monitoring the internal changes of the organization for the transition phases of the profiles used by the company to act in the face of market changes, because without this type of management the organization can lose its way and its identity during the various adaptations assigned throughout the process of existence.

This is why Culture Management is such an important model for the context experienced by companies, because the planned management of these changes must occur continuously and very intensely due to the market, and these alterations are necessary for the continuity of the company's activities, precisely because of the ability of the organizational culture to influence the application of strategies, either by making it impossible or by enhancing the level of adherence of employees to the culture. Still according to the same author, it is determined that by means of efficient

Culture is what makes it possible to associate the behavioral profile of employees with strategic objectives (ALHO; CARVALHO, 2007).

2.6.2.5 Organizational Climate Management

According to Flávio de Toledo and Benedito Milion (1986), Organizational Climate can be understood as a set of values, practices, attitudes and behavioural postures assumed within the organization, generally derived from the culture profile of the founders, which exist and are followed within the company.

A second definition for Organizational Climate, which in the opinion of Professor George H. Litwin, can be understood as the quality existing in the organizational environment perceived and experienced by employees, but this perception and experience will determine the level of results delivered by workers, depending on their alignment and satisfaction with the existing climate.

Therefore, it can be said that Climate Management has its role precisely in the overall diagnosis of the level of satisfaction with the work environment and how much this aspect can influence the operational performance of employees and consequently the company as a whole (ALHO; CARVALHO, 2007).

Going further, it can be said that Organizational Climate Management is concerned with the way in which employees perceive, understand and experience the existing practices defined by the existing environmental climate, reacting to them and carrying out their tasks in the most appropriate way possible (FISCHER, 2002).

Therefore, the technique used by organizations is the Organizational Climate Survey, as this makes it possible to measure the level of employee satisfaction and understand the level of adherence to the values, practices and guiding principles of the company's culture, making it possible to act through Organizational Climate Management to improve this aspect and enable gains in productivity and quality (FISCHER, 1996).

To this end, the Human Resources sector must provide full support in People Management activities, through Organizational Climate Management, in order to identify points of dissatisfaction and demotivation, areas of resistance to change, management and communication problems, lack of knowledge and lack of commitment to the strategy, among others (ALHO; CARVALHO, 2007).

Chapter 3

3 METHODOLOGY

In order to construct the work, in line with the objectives set, it was necessary to carry out research into theories that would help, from understanding the problem, defining the topic, to clarifying the models proposed by authors, but what was really critical for this study was the contextualization, through interpretation, of the models for the reality of diversity in people management.

In this way, the method and procedure applied in this research is characterized as a systematic literature review, which according to Clarke (2001) can be described as a set of systematic methods that seek to answer an initial question, to identify, select and criticize research related to the theme, concluding with a selective collection of data to be analyzed and included in the review itself.

With a clearer understanding of what a systematic literature review is, Greenhalgh (1997) defines it as a synthesis of primary studies that contains clearly explained objectives, materials and methods and that has been conducted according to a clear and reproducible methodology.

Based on these concepts, it can be said that a systematic literature review is a research model that investigates, by means of systematized methods of search, critical appraisal and synthesis, using the scientific literature on a given topic as a source of data (CLARKE, 2001).

Therefore, this theoretical study will be based on and elucidate the theme through theories that have already been defined and widely applied.

3.1 RESEARCH CHARACTERIZATION

Considering the methodological approach and according to Gil (2002), the research is exploratory in nature, as it contributes information and suggestions that allow for better familiarization with the subject, making it more explicit or enabling new hypotheses. It is also important to point out that one of the most important sources of research in this work is the documentary type, which made use of the database published in journal proceedings, with relevance in the area, to carry out the survey of data to be analyzed and has a quantitative and qualitative approach, which are present in the improvements of the results and in the final considerations according to Gil (2002).

In terms of subject matter, this study is essentially a bibliometric study, precisely because it uses theoretical research sources to support and also result in the most widely used models in journals (MEDEIROS, 2014).

This study was carried out through a survey of scientific theoretical material, and is characterized as explanatory, with qualitative and quantitative approaches.

The research is defined as explanatory because it is willing to devote considerable effort to theorizing, studying and reflecting on the objective to be achieved (MARCONI; LAKATOS, 2011).

The qualitative approach, according to Bradley (1993), is a form of study in which the researcher is an interpreter of reality, where the study data does not generate statistical information for inference, but an inductive evaluation, allowing the researcher to develop concepts, ideas and understandings based on a comparison previously made between the results of the study and the theoretical foundation (RENEKER, 1993).

It can also be described as a study with a quantitative approach, because according to Marconi and Lakatos (2011), quantification was used in the collection and treatment of data, using percentages to represent proportions found in the models investigated.

It is also characterized as being hypothetical-deductive (MARCONI; LAKATOS, 2011), as it consists of constructing propositions (hypotheses) that will be subjected to publicity (subjecting the subject to new criticism), in order to verify which hypotheses remain valid. The procedure for the study will be exclusively theoretical.

3.2 UNIVERSE AND SAMPLE

In order to delimit the study to a relevant sample, with an adequate degree of confidence, but still being a bibliographical review with the support of documentary research, as well as a bibliometric study, this work made use of a search in the annals of the publications of the last five (5) years, from 2010 to 2015, of the Journal of Contemporary Administration - RAC, which is linked to the National Association of Postgraduate Studies and Research in Administration - ANPAD.

In this way, 275 articles were found in this database, but when the search was applied using key words to identify and find articles related to the topic, 15 studies associated with the topic were found, which served as the basis for the survey of the models most used in Brazilian companies.

If we look at the numbers of material that was collected in order to carry out this research, we can see that the study was concluded by exploring 15 (fifteen) field studies carried out with Brazilian companies, with a total of 59 (fifty-nine) individual interviews carried out directly with members of these organizations, but also with a total of 2. 122 (two thousand one hundred and twenty-two) questionnaires applied indirectly to other members of these same companies.122 (two thousand one hundred and twenty-two) questionnaires applied indirectly to other members of these same companies and concluding that of these studies explored, more than 164 (one hundred and sixty-four) companies were studied on issues related to People Management in Brazil.

3.3 DATA COLLECTION PROCEDURE

The study used a systematic review of the literature on the subject, with the aim of elucidating what people and organization management is, but with a focus on the existing models of this type of management. In order to achieve the proposed objective, through the sample applied, documentary research was used through the categorization of these publications, but the use of keywords was applied in the sense of the proposed theme, such as people management model, Brazilian companies and people management.

The research was carried out by searching the index of volumes of the RAC annals over the years, and the search was made from volume 14 to volume 19, as they cover the period from 2010 to 2015. In each volume, the publication numbers appear, with each number corresponding to a certain period of months for the proposed year of each volume, and finally the articles option was selected, which allows us to check the keywords related to each article to see if they are pertinent to the subject of this study.

However, in order to obtain the information needed for the analysis, a basic procedure was used, developed by the author of this study himself, in which the literature review was fundamental, in which a basic, qualitative and representative model of the predominant characteristics of each People Management model was established, derived from the theoretical definitions discussed in this work and converted into characteristics.

This resulted in Table 1. This categorization model made it possible to visualize and practice the validation of the various types of people management models found in the studies captured by the research carried out in the RAC.

Table 1 - People Management Models and their main characteristics

	People Management Models	**Main feature**
Traditional People Management Models	**Classic**	Focus on the operational task by strict standards
	Motivational	Broader processes and employee well-being
	Strategic	Involved employees and customer focus
	Competitive	Adapted to demands and employees focused on continuous improvement

New People Management Models		
	Competence Management	Using individual skills to meet the organization's goals
	Knowledge Management and Learning	Development and use of constructive ideas as knowledge products
	Strategic change management	Ability to adapt in a programmed way, involving people in the change process
	Organizational Climate Management	Satisfaction management and alignment with the organizational culture to improve performance
	Organizational Culture Management	Aligning employee behavior with strategic objectives

Source. author (2016)

In this way, the research can be said to be through sources such as reference works and/or scientific journals, as the form of location is through the database of the annals of the RAC.

Chapter 4

4 ANALYSIS AND DISCUSSION

In order to focus on the main objective of this study, which was to analyze the People Management models described in the scientific literature, it is worth noting that the research carried out with the help of search tools allowed sufficient material to be found to meet the proposal, as already reported in the methodology, but it was also necessary to apply manual searches within the site itself, applying the search by keywords, so that it was possible to have sufficient material, since it is a relatively new theme and little explored in scientific studies applied to Brazilian companies.

For the study in question, the data processing aspect was very straightforward and simple, since the research was basically characteristic, through the collection of information that characterizes the models according to the definitions set out by the authors and the model built by the author of this study, but finally it was still possible to associate quantitative data, to better elucidate the proposal to verify the main People Management models in Brazilian companies.

The study was concerned with surveying and evaluating the People Management models found in case studies in Brazilian companies, so the validation went through critical verifications as to the preponderant characteristics of the models used in the companies of the studies surveyed, according to what was mentioned in the methodology and referring to Table 1, and it was through these that it was possible to associate the applied model, not least because considering the new People Management models as dimensions that are practiced simultaneously, but with greater or lesser weightings among them according to the reality experienced by the organization.

It is important to remember that the categorization of people management models was fundamental to this stage of the study. At first glance, after capturing the RAC articles by searching for the key words linked to people management, the means found to determine the association between the model used by a particular company in each study could not be defined other than by analyzing the characteristics found in the study and comparing them with the model established and represented in Table 1, thus considering a proposal that was fundamental to achieving the main objective of this work.

But what can be reported initially is that, according to studies carried out by Alho and Carvalho (2007), companies' approach to the application of modern forms of people management, not least due to the very use of the human resources sector, was very incipient about 10 years ago.

So, as a complement to the study carried out by the aforementioned author (ALHO; CARVALHO, 2007) and in order to elucidate the objective proposed for this study, observing the use of the new People Management models is perhaps the fundamental aspect for this work and critical for the moment experienced by organizations today, and from what has been described about the new models and the way it will be presented below in the study, it is important to understand that these new dimensions occur simultaneously in organizations, to a greater or lesser extent according to the context experienced by them.

Corroborating this line of thought, the idea of applying the new People Management models, as already defined and mentioned in topic 2.6.2, permeates among the traditional, strategic and competitive models, the application of practices related to the 5 (five) new dimensions of People Management, occurring in much the same way as represented in table 1, where one of these models can be used fully or the methods of more than one model can be applied simultaneously, but there will always be a preponderance of one of these new People Management models.

Chart 2 - New dimensions of People Management

Strategic				**Competitive**
⟵				⟶
Organizational Culture Management	**Knowledge Management and Learning**	**Organizational Climate Management**	**Competence Management**	**Strategic change management**

Source: adapted from Alho and Carvalho (2007)

It is important to note that there is no more or less correct model among the new dimensions of People Management. What actually happens is that each organization will have to apply the practices of one or other management model according to the moment and the needs of the market.

4.1 INFORMATION GATHERING

It is important to remember that the research in this study, in addition to targeting an important and strategic issue for Brazilian companies, also revealed initial practices aimed at the new people management models, but that this evidence was observed by the materials obtained for the scope, field and place where the research was carried out, which both the period and the source researched may have generated some limitation, but which is believed to be minimal, given the relevance of the source used and the fact that this topic is relatively new and little explored in field research.

4.2 ANALYSIS OF INFORMATION

Initially, an aspect considered common to practically all the cases researched was the fact that they believed in valuing the human factor as the foundation for the success of the company's results, where it was possible to see that in reality some of the managers used significant methods associated with the organizational climate, motivation, employee participation and involvement and cooperation, as management practices to manage their human resources, falling short of robust People Management models that could be used.

However, a relative number of organizations have shown, through the reports of managers and employees, that they have innovative practices in human resource management, which are associated with effective and new models applicable in this field. These approaches have shown, for example, that employees are involved in decision-making and their degree of freedom has increased.

A detailed list of the survey, other information and even the categorization of the models seen in the studies can be found in Table 3.

Table 3 - List of studies researched, information and categorization

AUTHOR AND YEAR	**KEY WORDS**	**CHARACTERISTIC FOUND**	**ASSOCIATED MODEL**
Tanure, Evans and Can^ado (2010)	People management and strategic people management.	Partner for change.	Strategic change management
Brandao et al. (2013)	People management.	Mapping the organizational culture to assess facilitating and hindering aspects.	Organizational Culture Management
Horta, Demo and Roure (2012)	People management policies, trust in the organization and well-being at work.	Involvement policies and training and development policies.	Knowledge Management and Learning
Sant'anna, Paschoal and Gosendo (2012)	Leadership and organizational support.	Professional relationships for well-being at work.	Organizational Climate Management

Pinho, Bastos and Rowe (2015)	Organizational bonds and organizational commitment.	Maximum commitment.	Classic People Management Model
Valladares, Vasconcellos and Serio (2014)	Innovativeness, innovativeness and determinants of innovativeness.	Transformational leadership, strategic understanding of innovation and managing people for innovation.	Strategic change management
Meirelles and Camargo (2014)	Dynamic capabilities, competencies and skills.	Skills management.	Competence Management
Turano and Cavazotte (2015)	Leadership.	Charismatic, Transactional and Transformational Leadership.	Organizational Culture Management
Moscardini and Klein (2015)	Corporate education and leadership.	Developing people to improve the skills considered critical to the business and promoting continuous learning.	Competence Management
Cruz, Frezatti and Bido (2015)	Leadership style, management control system and technological innovation.	Innovative and motivated by culture.	Strategic change management
Coda and Ricco (2010)	Behavioral style and strategic people management.	Committed and motivated.	Organizational Climate Management

Cruz, Sarsur and Amorim (2012)	Skills management and work relations.	Modern business and people management through the implementation of competency management systems.	Competence Management
Domingos and Neiva (2014)	Organizational change, organizational capacity for change and perception of change.	Planned and appropriate management for the changes.	Strategic change management
Marques et al. (2014)	Organizational change, work commitment and performance evaluation.	Commitment and perception of organizational change.	Organizational Culture Management
Maciel and Camargo (2013)	Satisfied, intending to leave and cooperative	People and career management have a direct influence on satisfaction, intention to leave and cooperative behavior.	Motivational People Management Model

Source: author (2016)

Therefore, as a way of commenting on some of the studies initially researched, in one of the cases studied (BRANDÁO et al., 2013), it was explained by the interviewees (employees) that one of the main competitive advantages is perceived to be the commitment and motivation of the teams. In this same case, an internal opinion poll also showed that there has been an increase in the level of employee satisfaction since management practices aimed at greater team engagement and motivation began to be practiced, rising from 55% in 2003 to 71% in 2004.

In another of the case studies researched (DOMINGOS; NEIVA, 2014), it was observed that the people management practices of those organizations seemed to show consideration for employees and the existing organizational culture. Practices were also observed that improved internal communication and that when there were changes in roles and procedures, there was always a well-planned transition period, using training and professional development techniques. In the case of this research, the Job Satisfaction and Organizational Climate factor stands out, as it was the most highly rated in the internal survey, whose items revealed employee satisfaction with the work they do and the pleasant working climate in the departmental teams.

In another case studied (HORTA; DEMO; ROURE, 2012), where people management practices were more focused on standardized management and associated with routine, activities focused on Human Resources Management policies were reported, which were incorporated by the organization in question, showing that the factor with the highest average was the working conditions policy, while the factor with the lowest average was the rewards policy. Therefore, in this case, it was assessed and confirmed that remuneration and incentive practices need to be reworked to ensure that the effort-reward relationship is practiced, fulfilled and rewarded clearly among all employees in order to avoid retaliatory attitudes.

Still for the same case cited in the previous paragraph, the study pointed out that three policies practiced by the organization have the potential to gain the trust of employees, being the rewards policy, the involvement policy and the training and development policy, which whenever the practices aimed at these are efficiently fulfilled, greater trust and involvement on the part of employees is soon perceived. So in this case study there was an interesting final consideration to share, which was the fact that when People Management policies are well propagated and adhered to within companies, they soon become powerful tools for influencing employee engagement and motivation, which can critically affect organizational performance.

In another case study (SANT'ANNA; PASCHOAL; GOSENDO, 2012), it was pointed out that the way of managing must adapt to the situation and the needs imposed by the market, a fact that was evidenced in the study in question. The important point raised in this case is the fact that the actions and behaviors of leaders have the power to influence the emotional states of employees and the work routine, but incredibly they are not related to the perception that life goals are being achieved and individual potentials are being expressed and developed. Remembering that this was what was observed in the case in question, but that for effective people management, the complete approach to the motivational aspects of employees must be relevant to the leadership posture.

In another study (PINHO; BASTOS; ROWE, 2015), the results surveyed and presented pointed to a focus on achieving maximum employee commitment, which was basically associated with the notions of involvement and motivation. The results indicated that the constructive involvement of employees with the organization, through continuous and sustainable practices, are the basis for this method of managing people.

Another study (VALLADARES; VASCONCELLOS; SERIO, 2014), aspects associated with human resource management methods in organizations extremely focused on innovation were addressed, where the important point made was that companies seeking to innovate in their products and processes must invest in the efficient communication of values and objectives related to innovation, These aspects must certainly be associated with the organizational culture of innovation-oriented companies, but for this whole process to be well practiced it is critical to realize that the main point is leadership and that their development must occur through learning and disseminating the organizational culture before any other process.

Finally, an interesting study (CODA; RICCO, 2010) that consolidates a very strong line of thought among the proposals of people management models, reports that even companies that are concerned with the motivational orientation of the team and tend to operate in the direction of strategic innovation, should have peculiar practices in the direction of the behavioral management of employees, with observance of changes in the organization, but with a very assertive basis in the organizational culture.

4.2.1 Presentation of Informales

According to the studies researched, the approaches presented and the characteristics extracted from them, but mainly based on the definitions previously presented in this work, it was possible to survey the information needed to characterize and associate the people management models found in the studies extracted from the annals of the Revista de Administragao Contemporánea - RAC over the last five (5) years, from 2010 to 2015, where it was possible to enrich this study with information related to management aspects used by companies, as well as methods associated by the Human Resources sectors and other information as already described and reported in Table 4 below.

Table 4 - Percentage of people management models surveyed

	People Management Models	%
Traditional People Management Models	Classic	7%
	Motivational	7%
	Strategic	40%
	Competitive	47%

Source: author (2016)

The results of this research, quantitatively represented in Table 4, made it clear that there is a considerable participation of organizations concerned with new methods of people management, since the number of organizations that were found using techniques focused on traditional models was around 14%, while modern methods accounted for the remaining 87%.

For modern people management models there is also an interesting observation, which is the intense participation in the application of techniques aimed at the competitive approach, which had a participation of 47%.

The most important contribution of this study was the possibility of categorizing and classifying the five (5) dimensions of the new people management models that were extracted from the 87% quantified from the strategic model and the competitive model (Table 5).

Table 5 - Percentage of new people management models surveyed

	People Management Models	%
New People Management Models	Competence Management	23%
	Knowledge Management and Learning	8%
	Strategic change management	31%
	Organizational Climate Management	15%
	Organizational Culture Management	23%

Source: author (2016)

According to Table 5, it is possible to carry out critical analyses and considerations for improving these shares according to the context experienced by the organizations, knowing that the application of these models is not necessarily what the company needs, but what it wants to apply in a certain market situation.

In this way, the preponderant characteristics of the people management practices in the organizations were also extracted, which made it possible to quantify the models, which have already been explained in topic 3.3 of this work, but just as important was that some intrinsic aspects of the Human Resources sectors of these organizations were also observed and how they were acting in the companies surveyed.

Some of the testimonies, practices and attitudes addressed by the companies' HRs determined, among the various cases, that the sector generally worked as a mere executor of labor practices or simply operational within the flow of people management processes that were practiced. However, it was also noted that this sector was integrating endomarketing itself, with a focus on clarifying and aligning the organizational culture for all employees.

The Human Resources sector also played a role in assessing the level of trust and motivation among employees, mediated by predetermined people management policies and practices. In certain cases it was possible to see that HR acted on two main fronts, one being in support of the management of the various sectors of the organization, with measures aimed at employees and their needs and well-being, and the other being in the process of attracting and retaining talent, acting in the operational and bureaucratic process that has historically always been the main function of this sector.

However, it was also possible, by observing the preponderant characteristics of people management, as well as the performance of human resources in the various cases studied, to list, in Table 6, the current and main challenges that companies face in correctly implementing an appropriate people management model.

Chart 6 - The main challenges of people management

1	Managing the organizational climate
2	Aligning people/skills with business strategy
3	Developing and training managers
4	Train, coach and develop people

5	Organizational Culture Management
6	Retaining talent
7	Supporting and promoting organizational change

Source: author (2016)

This study made it possible, through the information and data collected, to verify and validate the seven main characteristics that permeate people management models, a fact that was crucial to being able to quantify data and guarantee a quantitative perception of the presence of existing people management models and their use in Brazilian organizations.

FINAL CONSIDERATIONS

Initially, it is important to highlight the limitations that marked the development of the study, because although it contributed with fundamental and critical findings and their implications, some difficulties really limited the study, the main one stemming from the low number of articles pertinent to the concept of people management and its models, even though the research base is very relevant and supplied with a lot of material, but for the period and theme proposed it was laborious to find studies related to the theme of this work. Another problem was the issue of time to carry out the study, since it could perhaps have been richer in sources and research, even altering some of the methodological procedures, but the limitation of time complicates the researcher's ability to seek out more sources and work more on the issue of data and information for the study in question.

According to the proposal, the objective of the research that was carried out, based on the method that was commented on in the methodology, mentioned in topic 3.3, interesting aspects were observed, and it was possible to perceive the practice of People Management methods from traditional proposals to the most recent and efficient methods of models strategically suited to changes in the scenario, that is, it is notable that all People Management models, from the traditional to the most modern, are valid today.

Although studies on new people management models and the role of the new HR have advanced, research shows that most organizations have people management models that are inadequate for the challenges they face. However, in the vast majority of current cases, this is not due to a lack of interest, but due to a lack of internal training and preparation on the part of the organization itself to use appropriate strategic planning and the culture of dealing with people management and the participation of the human resources sector in a more efficient manner. This is so true that this study shows the interest of organizations in applying people management techniques and practices that are increasingly geared towards new trends, a fact that is on the rise due to the aggressiveness of the market and the new demands that are appearing faster and faster in the globalized world, which is also influencing the new behavioral profiles of today's professionals, which also influence the application of new models.

What was observed from the people management practices carried out by the HR sector of the organizations surveyed was that despite the interest and importance of applying activities geared towards modern people management models, there is an effort in the routine to work on important aspects geared towards the new trends in managing people, but it is still not a very sustainable proposal, due to the very way these activities are carried out, generally without priority or alignment with the strategic planning guidelines and consequently due to the importance, relevance, participation and autonomy that the HR sector has in the process as a whole in the organizations.

In this way, this study achieved its main objective by studying, characterizing and even quantifying the participation of existing people management models in Brazilian companies. We started from the idea that people management models are determined by studies over time and that they are in fact applicable in organizations, so much so that there are traditional models and new models, considered as such in these studies, but which can be seen in other studies as dimensions of the new people management models.

Through the theoretical studies carried out at the beginning of this work and the research carried out afterwards, with its cases over time and its theoretical references, it was not practical and simple to find direct definitions of the existing people management models, but there are several reports and characteristics that indirectly link to this theme, discussing a lot about leadership, practices and policies (operational and management) of People Management. Finally, it was realized that this subject is not so widely studied and addressed in theoretical and scientific materials, but by reaching the necessary theories in this study and with the clarification made, it was possible to elucidate about people management and its models. In this way, another very important and relevant contribution of this study was on the subject itself, through the study and research that was carried out on the proposed topic.

In this way, this work can contribute directly to the study carried out on the subject, but also because of the motivation it provides for the possibility of enriching studies on people management models and their contributions to modern organizations.

REFERENCES

ALHO, M. R.; CARVALHO, P. A. M. **INFORMATION TECHNOLOGY AND THE NEW PEOPLE MANAGEMENT MODELS.** 2007. 103 f TCC (Specialized), Fundagao Instituto de Administragao, Brasilia, 2007.

ÁVILA, L. V.;STECCA, J. P.; **People Management;** Santa Maria: Federal University of Santa Maria, Polytechnic College; 2015.

BECKER, B. E.; HUSELID, M. A.; ULRICH, D. **The Human Resource scorecard**: linking people, strategy, and performance; Harvard Business School Press, Boston - Massachusetts, 2001.

BRADLEY, J. **Methodological issues and practices in qualitative research**. Library Quarterly, v. 63, n. 4, p. 431-449, Oct. 1993. Available at: < http://www.journals.uchicago.edu/toc/lq/current>. Accessed on: Aug. 19, 2016.

BRANDÄO, H. P. et al. Gestao de Pessoas como Fator de Sucesso na Incorporagao da Nossa Caixa pelo Banco do Brasil. **Revista de Administragao Contemporánea**, Rio de Janeiro, v. 17, n. 5, p.598-619, Sep. 2013. Available at:< http://www.anpad.org.br/periodicos/content/frame_base.php?revista=1> Accessed on: Aug. 19, 2016.

BRANDÄO, H. P.; GUIMARÄES, T. A. Gestao de Competencias e Gestao de Desempenho. **Revista RAE**, FGV,v.41, n.1, jan./mar. 2001. Available at <http://rae.fgv.br/rae/vol41-num1-2001/>. Accessed on: Aug. 19, 2016.

CODA, R.; RICCO, M. F. F. Behavioral Styles of Science, Technology and Innovation (S,T&I) Professionals. **Revista de Administragao Contemporánea**, Curitiba, v. 14, n. 3, p.516-531, May 2010. Available at:< http://www.anpad.org.br/periodicos/content/frame_base.php?revista=1> Accessed on: Aug. 19, 2016, at 11:25.

CHIAVENATO, I. **Introduction to general management theory.** 6.ed. Rio de Janeiro: Campus, 2000.

. **People management: the new role of human resources in organizations.** Sao Paulo: Campus, 1999.

CRUZ, A. P. C.; FREZATTI, F.; BIDO, D. S. Leadership Style, Managerial Control and Innovation: The Role of Control Levers. **Revista de Administraçâo Contemporânea,** Rio de Janeiro, v. 19, n. 6, p.772-794, nov. 2015. Available at:< http://www.anpad.org.br/periodicos/content/frame_base.php?revista=1> Accessed on: Aug. 19, 2016.

CRUZ, M. V. G.; SARSUR, A. M.; AMORIM, W. A. C. Gestao de Competências nas Relaçôes de Trabalho: que Pensam os Sindicalistas? **Revista de Administraçâo Contemporânea,** Rio de Janeiro, v. 16, n. 5, p.705-722, Sep. 2012. Available at:< http://www.anpad.org.br/periodicos/content/frame_base.php?revista=1> Accessed on: Aug. 19, 2016.

DALMAU, M. B. L.; TOSTA, K. C. B. T.; **People Management Strategy**. Santa Catarina, 2009.

DOMINGOS, S. G.; NEIVA, E. R. Employees' Perception of Transactional and Transformational Change in a Public Organization. **Revista de Administraçâo Contemporânea**, Rio de Janeiro, v. 18, n. 2, p.118-138, mar. 2014. Available at:< http://www.anpad.org.br/periodicos/content/frame_base.php?revista=1> Accessed on: Aug. 19, 2016.

FARIA, M. de F. B.; **People Management**. INEPAD - INSTITUTO DE ENSINO E PESQUISA EM ADMINISTRAÇÂO; 2006.

FISCHER, A. L. **A conceptual and historical review of people management models. In: People in the organization.** Sao Paulo: Editora Gente, 2002.

FISCHER, A. L. **Possibilities and limits of qualitative methods in internal organizational research.** Paper presented at the Congreso Latinoamericano de Administración. Santiago/Chile, 1996.

FLEURY, M. T. L.; OLIVEIRA Jr., M. M. **Aprendizagem e gestâo do conhecimento.** In: FLEURY, Maria Tereza Leme (Coord.). As Pessoas na organizaçao. Sao Paulo: Gente, 2002.

FLEURY, A.; FLEURY, M. T. L. **Estratégias empresariais e formaçâo de competências**: um quebra cabeça kaleidoscópio da indústria brasileira. Sao Paulo: Atlas, 2000.

GIL, A. C. **Como elaborar projetos de pesquisa**. 4. Ed. Sao Paulo: Atlas Editora, 2002.

GREENHALGH, T. **Papers that summarize other papers (systematic review and meta-analyses)**. British Medical Journal, London, v. 315, n. 7109, p. 672-675, Sep. 1997.

HORTA, P.; DEMO, G.; ROURE, P. Políticas de Gestao de Pessoas, Confianza e Bem-estar: Estudo em uma Multinacional. **Revista de Administrado Contemporánea**, Rio de Janeiro, v. 16, n. 4, p.566-585, jul. 2012. Available at:< http://www.anpad.org.br/periodicos/content/frame_base.php?revista=1> Accessed on: Aug. 19, 2016.

LAKATOS, E. M.; MARCONI, M. A. **Metodología Científica**. 6. ed. Sao Paulo: Atlas Editora, 2011.

LEME, R. **Practical application of people management: mapping, training, selection, evaluation and measurement of results.** Rio de Janeiro: Qualitymark, 2005.

MACIEL, C. O.; CAMARGO, C. Overqualification at Work and its Influence on Attitudes and Behaviors. **Revista de Administraçao Contemporânea**, Rio de Janeiro, v. 17, n. 2, p.218-238, mar. 2013. Available at:< http://www.anpad.org.br/periodicos/content/frame_base.php?revista=1> Accessed on: Aug. 19, 2016.

MARQUES, A. L. et al. Relationships between Resistance to Change and

Organizational Commitment in Public Servants of Minas Gerais. **Revista de Administraçao Contemporânea**, Rio de Janeiro, v. 18, n. 2, p.161-175, mar. 2014. Available at:< http://www.anpad.org.br/periodicos/content/frame_base.php?revista=1> Accessed on: Aug. 19, 2016.

MEDEIROS, J. B. **Redado Científica**: a prática de fichamentos, resumos, resenhas. 12. ed. Sao Paulo: Atlas Editora, 2014

MEIRELLES, D. S.; CAMARGO, Á. A. B. Dynamic Capabilities: What Are They and How to Identify Them? **Revista de Administrado Contemporánea**, Rio de Janeiro, v. 18, p.41-64, dec. 2014. Available at:< http://www.anpad.org.br/periodicos/content/frame_base.php?revista=1> Accessed on: Aug. 19, 2016.

MOSCARDINI, T. N.; KLEIN, A. Corporate Education and Leadership Development in Multisite Companies. **Revista de Administraçâo Contemporánea**, Rio de Janeiro, v. 19, n. 1, p.84-106, jan. 2015. Available at:< http://www.anpad.org.br/periodicos/content/frame_base.php?revista=1> Accessed on: Aug. 19, 2016.

NONAKA, I.; TAKEUCHI, H. **Creação do conhecimento na empresa.** Rio de Janeiro: Campus, 1997.

PINHO, A. P. M.; BASTOS, A. V. B.; ROWE, D. E. O. Different Individual-Organization Bonds: Exploring Their Meanings among Managers. **Revista de Administraçâo Contemporânea**, Rio de Janeiro, v. 19, p.288-304, Oct. 2015. Available at:< http://www.anpad.org.br/periodicos/content/frame_base.php?revista=1> Accessed on: Aug. 19, 2016.

RENEKER, M. H. **A qualitative study of information seeking among members of an academic community: methodological issues and problems**. Library Quarterly, v. 63, n. 4, p. 487-507, Oct. 1993. Available at:

< http://www.journals.uchicago.edu/toc/lq/current>. Accessed on: Aug. 19, 2016.

RIBEIRO, A. L. **Gestâo de Pessoas**. Sao Paulo: Saraiva Editora, 2005.

SANT'ANNA, L. L.; PASCHOAL, T.; GOSENDO, E. E. M. Bem-estar no Trabalho: Relações com Estilos de Liderança e Suporte para Ascensao, Promoçao e Salários. **Revista de Administraçâo Contemporânea**, Rio de Janeiro, v. 16, n. 5, p.744-764, sep. 2012. Available at:< http://www.anpad.org.br/periodicos/content/frame_base.php?revista=1> Accessed on: Aug. 19, 2016.

SILVA, E. L. **Metodologia da pesquisa e elaboração de dissertaçâo**. 4. ed. rev. atual. Florianópolis: UFSC, 2005.

SILVA, J. R. G.; VERGARA, S. C. O significado da mudança: as percepções dos funcionários de uma empresa brasileira diante da expectativa de privatizaçao. **Revista de Administraçâo Pública.** Jan-Feb/2000, n.1, v.34. Rio de Janeiro: Getúlio Vargas Foundation. 1999.

SINEK, S. **Why?** - How to motivate people and teams to act. Sao Paulo: Saraiva Editora, 2012.

TACHIZAWA, T.; FERREIRA, V. C. P.; FORTUNA, A. A. M. **Gestao com pessoas: uma abordagem aplicada às estratégias** de **negócios.** 2. ed. Rio de Janeiro: FGV, 2001.

TANURE, B.; EVANS, P.; CANÇADO, V. L. As Quatro Faces de RH: Analisando a Performance da Gestao de Recursos Humanos em Empresas no Brasil. **Revista de Administraçao Contemporânea**, Curitiba, p.594-614, jul. 2010. Available at:< http://www.anpad.org.br/periodicos/content/frame_base.php?revista=1> Accessed on: Aug. 19, 2016.

TEIGA, A. J. **Gestao de Pessoas**. Curitiba: PR: IESDE Brasil; 2012.

TOLEDO, F. **Dicionário de Recursos Humanos.** Sao Paulo: Atlas, 1986.

TURANO, L. M.; CAVAZOTTE, F. Scientific Knowledge on Leadership: A Bibliometric Analysis of *The Leadership Quarterly* Collection. **Revista de Administraçao Contemporânea**, Rio de Janeiro, v. 20, n. 4, p.434-457, Aug. 2015. Available at:< http://www.anpad.org.br/periodicos/content/frame_base.php?revista=1> Accessed on: Aug. 19, 2016.

ULRICH, D. **The champions of human resources**: innovating for the best results. Sao Paulo: Futura, 2003.

ULRICH, D., YOUNGER, J., BROCKNAK, W., ULRICH, M. **Human Resource from the Outside** In: Six Competencies for the Future of Human Resources; McGraw Hill Professional, 2012.

VALLADARES, P. S. D. A.; VASCONCELLOS, M. A.; SERIO, L. C. Innovation Capacity: A Systematic Literature Review. **Revista de Administraçao Contemporânea**, Rio de Janeiro, v. 18, n. 5, p.598-626, Sep. 2014. Available at:< http://www.anpad.org.br/periodicos/content/frame_base.php?revista=1> Accessed on: Aug. 19, 2016.

VERGARA, S.C. **Research Projects and Reports in Administration**. 4.ed. Sao Paulo: Atlas, 2003.

VIANNA, I. O. A. **METODOLOGIA DO TRABALHO CIENTÍFICO**: Um enfoque didático da produgao científica. Sao Paulo: Editora EPU, 2001.

XAVIER, R. de A. P. **Gestao** de **Pessoas, na Prática**. Sao Paulo: Editora Gente, 2006.

MIX
Papier aus verantwortungsvollen Quellen
Paper from responsible sources
FSC® C105338

Printed by Books on Demand GmbH, Norderstedt / Germany